Comfort Verses
for the Divorced Christian

Comfort Verses

for the
Divorced Christian

Encouragement and Hope
Through the Tough Times

by Lynn Kinnaman

Published by Works by Design Publications,
a division of Works by Design, LLC

All scripture verses, unless otherwise indicated, are taken from the
New International Version (NIV), The Living Translation (NLT) or
The Message Bible (TMB) and are labeled as such.

… Take hold of my words
with all your heart:
keep my commandments
and you will live.

Proverbs 4:4 (NIV)

Introduction

What are Comfort Verses? They are those Bible verses that sustain us through the tough times, reminding us that God loves us no matter how we've messed up or how hurt we have been. They show us how to live in fullness and joy

When I was going through divorce, I felt alone and lost. My emotions were unpredictable, overwhelming, foreign to me. I didn't know who I was or what to do.

I needed a safe place. I needed to be loved and understood.

I needed comfort.

I discovered there is comfort out there – not the fleeting escape of drugs, alcohol or anything else that obliterates things for a moment – what I found was lasting comfort. Timeless strength.

I knew others could benefit from what I'd learned, so I collected these Comfort Verses for you, so that you, too, can find meaningful support that never fails.

There are four week's worth of daily readings because I like the idea of four weeks – it's a solid, symmetrical time frame. And frame is a good word in this context. Just like our faith in God is our foundation, spending time reading the Bible provides a framework for a strong life structure. This is _especially_ important when you are going through tough times, like divorce.

If you broke your leg, you wouldn't hop right back on it and try to walk or run. You would go through a process that includes a cast, or framework, to protect your leg and help it heal correctly. It's important not to bypass those steps because the result could be additional damage or further injury.

It's the same with your emotional healing.

Over the next four weeks I'm going to ask you to set aside a quiet time each day to meet with God. By the end of this program, you will have created a habit. Your daily routine will include time with God and my hope is you will continue the routine after the 28 days are over.

Each day has a bit of homework or action for you to take. I've made them small, for example, a single item or point to ponder. That doesn't mean you can't expand on my assignment, it just means I want to get you started with a baby step so it's easy to do. I suggest you get a small notebook in which to write, because it's been proven that hand-writing your thoughts can be therapeutic. Typing on the computer is not as effective as putting pen to paper.

It's not easy going through divorce. You may run into other people, even Christians - sometimes especially Christians - who reject you or condemn you because you are divorced. Remember that human beings, even the best ones, make mistakes.

God doesn't condemn you.

You are precious and valuable in his eyes. He has plans for you – plans that are amazing. Keep your focus on him and you'll come through this stronger, more compassionate, more loving and more lovable. You will glorify him as a healed individual in ways you never could before this happened.

Take God at his word to love and comfort you. Let him surround you like the warmth of the sun, bringing you out of the darkness and into the light.

For you were once darkness, but now you are light in the Lord. Live as children of light (for the fruit of the light consists in all goodness, righteousness and truth) and find out what pleases the Lord.
Ephesians 5:8-10 (NIV)

Blessings in your journey.
Lynn

DAY ONE
GOD CARES

The Lord is a refuge for the oppressed, a
stronghold in times of trouble.
Those who know your name will trust in you;
for you, Lord, have never forsaken those who seek you.
~Psalm 9:9-10 (NIV)

When you are in the depths of pain, you can feel like a small boat adrift in a sea of despair. As if everyone has abandoned, forgotten or turned against you, .

Your heart aches for a secure harbor where you can regroup and renew your strength.

God is the port you're looking for. He is your shelter from the world, a safe place for you in difficult times. He knows the challenges you're facing and he offers a respite from the madness.

This stronghold is available to you just by seeking him. Plugging in daily to the power source - God's word - and recharging your spiritual battery gives you the energy you need to get through your day of work, children, friendships, duties, bills and adversity.

Begin by trusting God. Believe he is with you, by your side every step. Know that you can lean on him. He has never forsaken anyone who has sought him out.

The Message Bible (TMB) restates the same verse this way:

God's a safe-house for the battered, a sanctuary during bad times. The moment you arrive, you relax; you're never sorry you knocked.

Today's assignment is to take him up on his word. Make God your stronghold in troubled times Find sanctuary in him and let yourself rest on his promises.

DAY TWO
GOD CAN HANDLE IT

God is a safe place to hide, ready to help when we need him.
We stand fearless at the cliff-edge of doom,
courageous in sea-storm and earthquake,
Before the rush and roar of oceans,
the tremors that shift mountains.
Jacob-wrestling God fights for us, God-
of-Angel-Armies protects us.
~Psalm 46:1-3 (TMB)

When bad things happen, sometimes all you want to do is hide. It's tempting to turn to escape avenues that aren't healthy, such as sex, drugs or alcohol. The problem is these are not safe havens. Even less harmful pursuits can serve as temporary fixes, but that doesn't make them a good choice. We saw yesterday how God is a sanctuary, and here's another verse that reminds us that God is a safe place.

He is powerful. A friend of mine was recently caught in a series of tornados and floods. As she left the area, the airplane rose to a elevation above the devastation and she could look down on the turbulence of the funnels, clouds and lightning. It was a spectacular view and one that affirmed for her that God is bigger than tornados.

He makes us fearless before the storms of life.

Today I'd like you to think about and write down a time when God was a safe haven for you. How did that feel?

14 - Comfort Verses

DAY THREE
WHEN IT SEEMS LIKE
ALL IS AGAINST YOU

Count on it: Everyone who had it in for you
will end up out in the cold- real losers.
Those who worked against you will end up empty-handed-
nothing to show for their lives.

When you go out looking for your old
adversaries you won't find them-
Not a trace of your old enemies, not even a memory.
That's right. Because I, your God, have a firm
grip on you and I'm not letting go.
I'm telling you, "Don't panic. I'm right here to help you."
~Isaiah 41:11-13 (TMB)

When you are going through rough times, it can feel like no one is on your side. A divorce robs you of your spouse and can cost you friends. Your family sometimes withdraws or can't cope. You're scared and alone.

People can be mean and hurtful. You wonder how life can be so unfair and inequitable. How can wickedness thrive while you suffer?

You might be tempted to try to even the score yourself, thinking no one else will. But don't be fooled. Evil will be punished, but God will be the one making the judgments. It's not your job and you don't have to spend time getting revenge. You have more important things to do.

You are in the firm grip of God and his justice is perfect, even if you aren't able to see how it all unfolds.

The New International Version (NIV) says the same verse like this:

> All who rage against you will surely be ashamed and disgraced; those who oppose you will be as nothing and perish. Though you search for your enemies, you will not find them. Those who wage war against you will be as nothing at all. For I am the LORD, your God, who takes hold of your right hand and says to you, Do not fear; I will help you.

He can vanquish your enemies and those who wage war, but it will be in his time and place. We don't have to worry about justice because he is in charge of it all. Today's assignment is to take a situation, big or small, where your instinct is to seek revenge but you are willing to lay it at God's feet and let him handle it.

Then let it go.

DAY FOUR
<u>FEAR NOT</u>

> *So we say with confidence,*
> *"The Lord is my helper; I will not be afraid.*
> *What can man do to me?"*
> *~Hebrews 13:6 (NIV)*

Sometimes it feels like "man" can do a lot, and it seems there are many things to fear. You might be afraid you won't have a place to live, or money to pay the bills, or that your car might fall apart, or that you will never be loved again.

These fears might be rational. Or they might be like a panic attack - feeling real but with no basis in fact.

Either way, if you make room for them in your life fears are delighted to move in and take over. They will dictate your decisions, taint your relationships and hamstring your progress.

When you feel fear, you can be confident it's not from God. In fact, one of the most frequent commands in the Bible is to "fear not". Our Creator knows how destructive fear can be, and he has the antidote.

He IS the antidote.

God is calling us to reject fear and find courage. The dictionary defines courage this way:

- the ability to do something that frightens one: she called on all her courage to face the ordeal,
- strength in the face of pain or grief: he fought his illness with great courage.

You have God's help, encouragement and support to do this. Banish fear and live boldly, secure in the knowledge that this is part of God's plan for you.

Write down one fear you will replace with trust.

DAY FIVE
<u>REST ASSURED</u>

*You can go to bed without fear;
you will lie down and sleep soundly.
You need not be afraid of sudden disaster
or the destruction that comes upon the wicked,
for the Lord is your security. He will keep
your foot from being caught in a trap.*
Proverbs 3:24-26 (NLT)

With so much going wrong in the world, and turbulence in your own life, a good night's sleep can be elusive. The act of laying down on your bed can unleash a string of thoughts you may have been able to hold at bay during the busy day.

Scenarios of disaster or destruction unfold like a 3D movie, and instead of relaxing, you become tense and wide awake.

You'd give a lot for a sound sleep, free of fears. Proverbs 3 tells us that wisdom will ease our sleep, and we can gain wisdom by keeping the teachings and commandments of the Lord. This chapter is full of great advice and precious guidance.

Today I'd like you to read Proverbs 3, pick one thing you intend to practice and write down how you will do that.

20 - Comfort Verses

DAY SIX
MANAGING YOUR THOUGHTS

Those who are dominated by the sinful nature think about sinful things, but those who are controlled by the Holy Spirit think about things that please the Spirit. So letting your sinful nature control your mind leads to death. But letting the Spirit control your mind leads to life and peace.
Romans 8:5-6 (NLT)

When you're going through difficult times, it's hard to control your thoughts. You might be thinking of revenge, worried about your future, fearing a decision by a judge, letting hate simmer like an evil stew.

Your thoughts plague you. You might feel like you can't control them. But you can. Not instantly, and maybe not without some serious practice, but you can control them.

I don't think the battle to control our thoughts is new. Paul wrote to the Philippians (4:8 NIV);

Finally, brothers, whatever is true, whatever is noble, whatever is right, whatever is pure, whatever is lovely, whatever is admirable—if anything is excellent or praiseworthy—think about such things.

One proven technique to manage your thoughts is to replace them with something positive. If you watch or read too much news, you know how it can drag you down. Imagine spending the bulk of your days thinking about things that are true, excellent and lovely.

Your challenge today is to write down at least three things that are true, excellent and lovely, then shift your focus to them when your mind begins to dwell on unwanted thoughts.

DAY SEVEN
<u>GRATITUDE LISTS</u>

Always giving thanks to God the Father for everything,
in the name of our Lord Jesus Christ.
Ephesians 5:8 (NIV)

One thing that will help you in controlling your thoughts and bring you more happiness is to keep a gratitude list. Researchers have found people who consider things daily for which they are grateful are happier, healthier and have better relationships.

The studies had people list five things they were grateful for every night before they went to sleep and found that, within a short time, the participants reported greater well-being and a more positive outlook. The researchers only confirm what God teaches; that giving thanks is a constant act that benefits us and glorifies God.

It's similar to what we learned yesterday, confirming Paul's advice that it's best to dwell on that which is good and true. Happiness follows. And in case you wonder if God wants you to be happy, consider this:

Be joyful always; pray continually; give thanks in all
circumstances, for this is God's will for you in Christ Jesus.
1 Thessalonians 5:16-18 (NIV)

Giving thanks even when life is a struggle is what God wants. Being joyful and praying is what God wants. Researchers have now proven that what God wants for us improves our lives.

It should be no surprise.

Starting today and continuing through the next three weeks, make a list every night before you go to sleep of five things for which you are grateful.

DAY EIGHT
WORRY IS A WASTE OF TIME

*Therefore do not worry about tomorrow, for
tomorrow will worry about itself.
Each day has enough trouble of its own.
~Matthew 6:34 (NIV)*

It's said that 90% of the things we spend time worrying about never happen. Yet it's where we often camp out, knee deep in fabricated fears and self-inflicted stress. Does all that worrying accomplish anything?

Worrying has been compared to sitting in a rocking chair; it gives you something to do but you never get anywhere.

It's a close cousin to fear, and it's one way people deal with their fears, as if worry can gnaw fear down to a manageable size. Unfortunately the only thing worry wears away is your health and well-being. The best advice I heard about worrying was; examine the situation or concern, determine if you can do something about, then do it. If you can't do anything about it, set it aside. Don't worry about what hasn't yet happened.

Another friend phrased it like this - *stay where your feet are.*

That's not to say you should stop being responsible. Don't run up a huge credit card bill and justify it by saying you simply don't worry about the future anymore. You shouldn't stop saving money, brushing your teeth or planting a garden, because these things will reap benefits later. The point is you shouldn't spend precious time fretting over what hasn't yet, or might never, happen.

I have this quote by Corrie ten Boom taped to my mirror. Corrie survived the holocaust and knew something about worry and fear of the future and she said this:

> *Worry does not empty tomorrow of its sorrow;*
> *it empties today of its strength.*

This quote touches my heart, especially coming from a woman who had so much personal devastation.

Jesus put it in perfect perspective when he asked if anyone can add one hour to his life by worrying. Well?

Of course no one can.

He goes on to say, if you can't add a single hour to your life by worrying, why do you bother worrying about anything? It's a plain fact you aren't going to be able to change it.

Today I'd like you to write down a worry that you have that has not happened and you know probably won't. Then feed it to the shredder or burn it in the fire pit, releasing it to God.

DAY NINE
WHAT TO DO
INSTEAD OF WORRYING

Don't worry about anything; instead, pray about everything.
Tell God what you need, and thank him for all he has done.
Then you will experience God's peace, which
exceeds anything we can understand.
His peace will guard your hearts and
minds as you live in Christ Jesus.
Philippians 4:6-7 (NLT)

The thing about worry is it gives us something to do. Like a dog with a bone, we can work at it until our jaw aches. Unlike the dog and bone, we don't gradually make it smaller through our efforts. For us, it's more like a rock, breaking our teeth and refusing to yield.

If you quit worrying, what will you do instead? Fortunately we have good advice. Pray about everything. Talk to God about your needs, your concerns, your fears. Thank him for everything he's done, and recognize he has blessed you in the midst of this situation.

What will you get when you do this? The answer to all your prayers?

It doesn't say that. However, you will get peace. An amazing peace. A peace allows you to function at your best, knowing God has your back. He guards your heart and your mind as you go through your days.

Today I'd like you to take another worry and pray about it. Tell God everything, and thank him.

Let it go.

Then let his peace flow over you.

DAY TEN
TRUSTING GOD IS KEY

But blessed is the man who trusts in the
LORD, whose confidence is in him.
He will be like a tree planted by the water that
sends out its roots by the stream.
It does not fear when heat comes; its leaves are always green.
It has no worries in a year of drought
and never fails to bear fruit.
Jeremiah 17:7-8 (NIV)

It seems everything we use today has a battery, and a limited battery life. The computer I'm using right now is fully charged, but over the course of the day will run down until I need to recharge it.

I charge my cell phone every night, but occasionally I use it so much the battery gets low in the middle of the day. When that happens, if I haven't been paying attention to the signal, it quits on me. Goes dead. It's useless until I plug it in and get it recharged.

Trusting in God, putting your confidence in him, is like connecting to our power source. We never want to be too far from it, because with a steady supply of energy, we can flourish. In the tough times, if we are plugged in, we will survive. Not only survive, but be fruitful and productive.

The things we have discussed to this point are all ways you can invest your confidence in God. Spend time with him. Talk to him. Study his Word.

Today I'd like you to keep practicing the lessons we've learned so far, and don't forget your gratitude list.

DAY ELEVEN
GOD PROVIDES

*Then, turning to his disciples, Jesus said,
"That is why I tell you not to worry about everyday life—
whether you have enough food to eat or enough clothes to wear.
For life is more than food, and your body more than clothing.
Look at the ravens. They don't plant or harvest
or store food in barns, for God feeds them.
And you are far more valuable to him than any birds!"*
Luke 12:22-24 (NLT)

We spend a lot of time fretting over whether we have enough. It's a hot button for me. For whatever reason, somewhere in my formative years I felt a fundamental lack and the seed of fear was planted. Would there be enough? What if it ran out before my turn? Would I be taken care of?

Jesus assures us that God provides. He cares for the smallest creatures in his world, and we are worth more to him than they are.

It's important to note that the birds don't simply sit on the ground, confident that God will give them everything. They forage for food, build nests, raise young – in other words, go about their lives. We need to go about our lives, too, but remember to keep God in the center of it all.

*So do not worry, saying, 'What shall we eat?' or 'What
shall we drink?' or 'What shall we wear?' For the pagans
run after all these things, and your heavenly Father knows*

that you need them. But seek first his kingdom and his righteousness, and all these things will be given to you as well.
Matthew 6: 31-33 (NIV)

Keep your priorities straight. Put God first and God will provide for you. He knows what you need.

Take a moment today to write about what worries you might have been putting ahead of God. Reorganize your priorities so that your first focus is on God and practice trusting him. Write about how this will look in your life.

DAY TWELVE
TRUE RECOVERY

Come to me, all you who are weary and
burdened, and I will give you rest.
Matthew 11:28 (NIV)

TMB says it this way:

Are you tired? Worn out? Burned out on religion?
Come to me. Get away with me and you'll recover
your life. I'll show you how to take a real rest.
Walk with me and work with me-watch how I
do it. Learn the unforced rhythms of grace.
I won't lay anything heavy or ill-fitting on you.
Keep company with me and you'll
learn to live freely and lightly.

If you seek complete recovery, know that it's possible with God. People can help, church can provide fellowship, recovery groups and coaching gives you a place to speak out and get guidance, but the true healing is within, a place that's only accessible to you and God.

His promise is like an oasis for your broken heart . . . your damaged ego . . . your hungry spirit. He is inviting you to bring it all to him. Trade it in for rest and peace. Not only that, but he will gently teach you what you need to know, being careful not to overload you or encumber you with something that's not right for you.

Wouldn't you like to learn the unforced rhythms of grace? It sounds lovely, doesn't it? Like an effortless dance of life in the arms of your Lord.

Would you like to live freely and lightly? With respite from your burdens? What a blessing that would be! And it's within your grasp. God doesn't promise to remove all difficulties, but he does offer to share them, easing the load.

Today let God take the weight off your shoulders. Walk with him, work with him to learn his ways. What's one thing God can teach you today?

DAY THIRTEEN
GRIEVING YOUR LOSS

For everything there is a season,
a time for every activity under heaven.
A time to be born and a time to die.
A time to plant and a time to harvest.
A time to kill and a time to heal.
A time to tear down and a time to build up.
A time to cry and a time to laugh.
A time to grieve and a time to dance.
Ecclesiastes 3:1-4 (NLT)

God provides powerful help, but maybe you still hurt. You might wonder why you are feeling such overwhelming heartache and misery from your divorce. Others have told you that divorce is common and you need to just get over it. And yet, the sorrow is in your bones, deep and painful.

Having faith in God doesn't mean you aren't going to experience human despair. He comes alongside to help you through it, but you still must acknowledge and respect the emotions you feel in order to be able to move past them.

No matter what your marriage was like, you once had hopes and dreams that it would be wonderful. You had visions of what your life would be like with that special person; perhaps raising children or growing old together. When the marriage died, the dream died. And the loss is as real as any literal death.

You are grieving.

You might tempted to try to dodge the pain or dismiss your feelings, thinking that by minimizing what you've lost you can box it up and stick it on a shelf where you can ignore it.

Remember the broken leg? You would be foolish to look at it and say "it's nothing, other people have gone through worse, I'm going to just go on with my life", then step out as if your leg was sound.

A wise person recognizes the reality of the broken leg, or broken heart, and responds accordingly. Your life has changed. There will be a time to move on, and a time to dance again, but right now it's okay for you to cry and grieve.

Your sadness is valid and normal. Give yourself permission to feel your feelings even if it's scary. Allow whatever time it takes to go through it. Be kind to yourself, as you would be to a friend.

Of course, if you find you are slipping into serious or clinical depression, don't hesitate to get professional help. God has much to offer us as we go through difficulties, and sometimes he offers it in the form of other people.

Give yourself a hug today and let you be you.

DAY FOURTEEN
GOD HEARS YOUR CALL

I love the Lord because he hears my
voice and my prayer for mercy.
Because he bends down to listen, I will
pray as long as I have breath!
Psalm 116:1-2 (NLT)

Have you ever called a company for help and gotten trapped in voice-mail wasteland? Press this button for that, that button for this, all the while they assure you that they value your business. Sure they do. The feeling I get is that they value my money, but really don't want to have to talk to me.

Listening is not only polite, it's required if you are going to have a meaningful relationship. God wants a meaningful relationship with you. Not one where you get his pre-recorded message, but one where he leans down to catch the words you speak. What a picture that creates in my mind!

Loving parents, attentive and focused, bend toward their children to hear every word. It may be nonsense, but it's important to that parent.

The NIV says it this way; *He turned his ear to me, He heard my voice.*

We don't pray to a stone god, a picture or a plastic figure, we pray to a living God, who hears us. Who wants to have a relationship.

When you pray today, know that God is listening. Pour out your heart. He hears your cry, and you can call on him forever.

What do you want to say to him?

DAY FIFTEEN
<u>GOD'S PEACE</u>

I am leaving you with a gift—peace of mind and heart.
And the peace I give is a gift the world cannot give.
So don't be troubled or afraid.
John 14:27 (NLT)

Everyone likes gifts. The promise, in the shiny box or pretty paper, of your heart's desire. The anticipation of revealing the treasure inside.

Our gifts to each other are usually material things, some longed for, others practical or necessary. Some gifts are a combination of both.

The gift of peace is an amazing thing. The dictionary defines peace as;
- freedom from disturbance
- serenity
- mental calm

People search the world for peace of mind and heart, yet it's not in any location or building or physical pose, it's in you, a gift that Jesus, speaking for God, has left for us.

You will keep in perfect peace all who trust in you,
all whose thoughts are fixed on you!
Trust in the Lord always,
for the Lord God is the eternal Rock.
Isaiah 26:3-4

Perfect peace can be yours. Peace of mind and heart. It's a gift. For you. Unwrap it today and hold it close. How will your life change when you have peace of mind and heart?

DAY SIXTEEN
QUIET TIME

Be still, and know that I am God;
I will be exalted among the nations,
I will be exalted in the earth.
Psalm 46:10 (NIV)

Being still is not one of my talents. While I acknowledge that multitasking is just a myth I'm not willing to give up on it quite yet. My days are full and my schedule is planned weeks in advance. Busy is my middle name.

Without a burning bush or pillar, how will I hear God? I won't, unless I take the time to be still and know he is God. Unless I quiet my hectic day and listen.

Prayer time is also meditation time. The word meditation has become entwined with a specific mind set that carries a negative connotation for many Christians. Yet the word meditation means:

- to focus one's mind for a period of time
- to think deeply or carefully about (something)

How you focus or think deeply and carefully can vary. Certain verses in the Bible suggest we meditate on the law day and night. I usually read a passage and consider a specific scripture. The important thing is to be still at some point and listen for God.

May my meditation be pleasing to him,
as I rejoice in the LORD.
Psalm 104:34

Rejoice in God and let your thoughts, your focus, your meditation be pleasing to him today. What verse or thought about God can you focus on or think deeply about in the next 24 hours?

DAY SEVENTEEN
<u>YOUR REFUGE</u>

I run for dear life to God, I'll never live to regret it.
Do what you do so well:
get me out of this mess and up on my feet.
Put your ear to the ground and listen,
give me space for salvation.
Be a guest room where I can retreat;
you said your door was always open!
You're my salvation—my vast, granite fortress.
Psalm 71:1-3 (TMB)

We've already talked about how God is our refuge and how he gives us the strength we need to live our lives. But it bears repeating.

Sometimes when we are into the Word and trying to get close to God, obstacles will arise to distract and discourage us. You might have had some things come up in the past few weeks that are especially challenging and you might be wondering how you are going to handle everything going on in your life.

It's a good time to remember who God is and how he is here for us. He can get us on our feet when we have no hope and can't form a plan. He gives us space and is always available.

You can run to God, he is waiting with open arms. He delights in being there for you and being your rock of refuge. He wants to rescue and deliver you from worldly predicaments.

What might be plaguing you? What are you finding unbearable? Write it down, then make it a point to turn to him before you consider any other option.

You'll never regret it.

DAY EIGHTEEN
FAITH IS A SOLID FOUNDATION

> *The fundamental fact of existence is that*
> *this trust in God, this faith,*
> *is the firm foundation under everything*
> *that makes life worth living.*
> *It's our handle on what we can't see.*
> *The act of faith is what distinguished our*
> *ancestors, set them above the crowd.*
> *Hebrews 11:1-2 (TMB)*

In the beginning of this series, I talked about building a framework of support to help you heal and recover from life's setbacks. Here you see that faith, trusting God, is the foundation upon which everything else stands.

A strong foundation is crucial to the stability and durability of a structure, and the foundation of your life should not be on shifting sands like money, other people, jobs or status.

I went through a period in my life where everything I had thought defined me crumbled. I lost my standing, my finances, my friends, my identity. Nothing remained except me, and I wasn't feeling too worthwhile. I was down to bare metal and had to figure out who I was and what life I intended to live.

It was, to say the least, humbling.

But priceless.

Because when you lose everything you once took for granted you have the unique opportunity to begin again, rebuilding a life that reflects who you really are. Rebuilding on a firm foundation.

Faith.

A life built on faith in God is truly a life worth living. And it's yours for the taking.

There are very few things that are unshakable. None that I can think of, except for God. I don't want to spend time investing in something that could be here today and gone tomorrow. What about you?

Today take a moment to examine your foundation. Does it set you above the crowd?

DAY NINETEEN
DEEP ROOTS EQUAL
STRONG TREES

Then Christ will make his home in your
hearts as you trust in him.
Your roots will grow down into God's love and keep you strong.
And may you have the power to understand,
as all God's people should,
how wide, how long, how high, and how deep his love is.
May you experience the love of Christ, though
it is too great to understand fully.
Then you will be made complete with all the fullness
of life and power that comes from God.
Ephesians 3:17-19 (NLT)

Another way to look at your foundation is to consider the roots of a tree. We look at trees from the ground up and admire their foliage and branches. But the real action is beneath our feet. Trees gain nourishment from their roots. Trees with strong roots are healthy trees.

When you make room in your heart for Jesus, he fills the empty space. It takes trust to make room. It takes leaning on him in tough times and giving thanks in all times.

The dictionary says trust means;
- to be sure of
- to commit to
- to count on

When you count on God, his presence grows. Your roots dig into him for stability and strength. You begin to get a glimpse of how immense his love is and your life expands.

No person can meet that need like God can. If you look for another romantic relationship before you develop your relationship with God, you're not going to get the satisfaction in your life you seek.

God makes your life complete. Seek him first and he will bring you what you long for.

> *Delight yourself in the LORD and he will*
> *give you the desires of your heart.*
> Psalm 37:4 (NIV)

Write down what some of the desires of your heart. Not your wish list, not your material desires, but the true desires of your heart.

DAY TWENTY
<u>MORE THAN JUST WORDS</u>

But don't just listen to God's word. You must do what it says.
Otherwise, you are only fooling yourselves.
For if you listen to the word and don't obey, it
is like glancing at your face in a mirror.
You see yourself, walk away, and forget what you look like.
But if you look carefully into the perfect
law that sets you free, and
if you do what it says and don't forget what you heard,
then God will bless you for doing it.
James 1:22-25 (NLT)

When my children were growing up there were times they grew weary of my parental guidance. I remember one instance when they were young and we had the discussion that goes on in every household.

Clean your room, I'd say. *Okay*, came the reply. An hour later I'd go check on things to find them playing with toys. *Clean your room now!* I'd repeat. *OKAY!* They'd say again.

An hour later, same thing. No change.

They heard me. They agreed with me. But they did nothing about it and the room remained a mess.

It's the same for us. It's not enough to read the Bible. It's not enough to be able to quote scripture. God knows the difference between lip service and true obedience.

He knows the intent of your heart.

When you study God's word, you want it to stick. You want to put it into action.

TMB puts it like this:

> *Don't fool yourself into thinking that you are a listener when you are anything but, letting the Word go in one ear and out the other. Act on what you hear! Those who hear and don't act are like those who glance in the mirror, walk away, and two minutes later have no idea who they are, what they look like. But whoever catches a glimpse of the revealed counsel of God—the free life!—even out of the corner of his eye, and sticks with it, is no distracted scatterbrain but a man or woman of action. That person will find delight and affirmation in the action.*

Review the truths you've learned the past three weeks and select a few (for starters) that you will act on today, this week and this year.

DAY TWENTY-ONE
FORGIVENESS IS POWERFUL

Bear with each other and forgive whatever
grievances you may have against one another.
Forgive as the Lord forgave you.
Colossians 3:13 (NIV)

Forgiveness is not optional. God expects us to forgive. He also knows how difficult it can be.

You've been wronged. It's human nature to harbor resentment and anger toward the person who treated you badly. It's human nature, but God wants us to strive for more than mere human response.

Forgiveness is possible because we are forgiven. Because Jesus died on the cross for our sins, the sacrifice was made and we were forgiven. He died in our place, yet all we have to do is to believe and accept him as our savior. We don't have to do penance or give any sacrifice of our own. We don't need to earn our salvation. It's by the grace of God, a pure gift. We only have to accept it.

For God loved the world so much that he gave his
one and only Son, so that everyone who believes
in him will not perish but have eternal life.
John 3:16 (NLT)

We've all done wrong. No matter how hard you struggle to live a good life, be a good person, sometime, someplace you're going to mess up. Maybe you've messed up in big ways. If we had to pay for every infraction, we'd have a debt it would take several lifetimes to eliminate. But Jesus died and wiped it out. Forgave it. Freed us.

One thing he asks is for us to forgive others. In case you wonder how much we should forgive, he says; *Forgive as we are forgiven.*

Maybe you just can't imagine it. Maybe your pain is so deep, your hurt so scarring that you don't think forgiveness is possible.

If you're not ready to make the decision to forgive - and forgiveness is a decision, not a feeling - begin by asking God to give you the desire to forgive and work your way towards it. God recognizes your willingness to consider it and sees you are taking steps to get there. He'll help you.

Who in your life does God wants you to forgive? Do you feel far from that step?

Begin by writing your intention. Then ask God for His power and strength.

DAY TWENTY-TWO
LOVING OTHERS

Do not seek revenge or bear a grudge
against one of your people,
but love your neighbor as yourself. I am the LORD.
Leviticus 19:18 (NIV)

Some people are easy to love. My children. My grandchildren. My sons-in-law and their families.

Others are almost impossible.

We've been taught that it's wrong to love yourself, but if you're not supposed to love yourself, how would this verse make any sense? God knows we love ourselves, we take care of ourselves and we maintain ourselves. What he's saying is he wants us to bring that same level of care to others. He wants us to consider their needs and their circumstances the same way we consider our own.

He also warns against holding grudges or seeking revenge. This is so much harder to do than it sounds. It's my opinion that of all the things God asks of us, this is one of the most difficult. It offends our sensibilities to be told we must love everyone, even our enemies.

I'm also convinced that's exactly why it's so important to him. What better measure of faith and trust than loving those who you don't even like?

Loving isn't the same as trusting and you can love without taking foolish chances. God wants you to love others, he doesn't say that they will be kind and loving toward you.

Love with intention, without expectation.

If you do, in true God fashion, blessings will follow.

You've heard stories of people whose lives have been radically changed by love. People who never felt valued discover they are loved and it turns their world on its head. Imagine, if everyone consciously practiced loving one another, how different things would be?

Who comes to mind? Throw love at them like rose petals. See what happens.

DAY TWENTY-THREE
<u>REACH OUT</u>

Therefore encourage one another and build each other up,
just as in fact you are doing.
1 Thessalonians 5:11 (NIV)

Encouragement is important, especially when people are struggling. When Paul wrote this letter to the Thessalonians, they were facing some of the same challenges Christians are today. There was dissension between believers and difficulties with non-believers. Paul wanted to recognize the value of their support and encouragement for each other.

For the past three-plus weeks, you've been leaning into God, relying on His promises and strength. Now it's time to exercise and test the new strength you've gained.

Keep your eyes open for someone around you whom you can love and fortify. Is there someone you can build up, in an honest and authentic way? Is there a friend who needs an encouraging word? Positive feedback?

Is there someone who has done much for you, but you forgot to thank?

Do it now.

When you are going through divorce or other trying times, you tend to meet others battling similar situations or life-challenges. When you do, take the opportunity to minister to them and yourself at the same time. That's right. Supporting others reflects back into your own life and gives you a lift, too.

By taking even tiny steps to reach out you are moving toward healing and recovery. It's like physical therapy for that broken leg. It's part of the overall process.

Write down names of those whom you can love and support. Someone who's facing their own challenges and could use a kind word. Then take action.

DAY TWENTY-FOUR
CONTINUING EDUCATION

These are the proverbs of Solomon, David's son, king of Israel.
Their purpose is to teach people wisdom and discipline,
to help them understand the insights of the wise.

Their purpose is to teach people to live
disciplined and successful lives,
to help them do what is right, just, and fair.

These proverbs will give insight to the simple,
knowledge and discernment to the young.
Proverbs 1:1-4 (NLT)

Most professions require continuing education credits. It's a way to ensure the person is well-educated in their field and has thorough knowledge. We need continued education, too. We need to keep inputting vital information.

The Bible is our textbook, God's guidelines for living.

Reading it not only brings us closer to God, we gain practical instruction on what our lives should look like.

In Proverbs 2 it says to seek wisdom, search for it like you would for precious gems. Wisdom will enter your heart and knowledge will fill you with joy. Your choices and understanding will keep you safe. Proverbs 3 tells you that if you trust in the Lord and seek his will in what you do, he'll show you what path to take.

You can see how important this continuing education is to your life.

We are four days from the completion of this series. This is a good time to make a plan to continue your education so you won't be left high and dry when you finish this book. Proverbs is a good place to begin.

Today, create a reading schedule that you can start as soon as Comfort Verses ends. As you read, plan to ask yourself questions about what you've read so you get the most from it.

CHAPTER TWENTY-FIVE
GOD KNOWS YOU AND LOVES YOU

You made all the delicate, inner parts of my body
and knit me together in my mother's womb.
Thank you for making me so wonderfully complex!
Your workmanship is marvelous—how well I know it.
You watched me as I was being formed in utter seclusion,
as I was woven together in the dark of the womb.
You saw me before I was born.
Every day of my life was recorded in your book.
Every moment was laid out before a single day had passed.
Psalm 139:13-16

If anyone really knew me, they wouldn't like me.

If you've ever had this thought, guess what?

You're human.

We present our best face to the world, but it doesn't always tell the whole story. And that's appropriate in certain situations.

I don't know about you, but if I get a brand-new doctor when I go to the emergency room, I don't want him telling me he's scared, or that he's never done this before or he isn't sure how to diagnose my ills.

I want confidence.

If I listen to a keynote speaker, I don't want apologies because his power-point didn't load, or he lost his notes, or he has a case of nerves because it's the first time he's spoken in front of such a large group. If he wants my attention for the next hour, at least ACT like a professional.

Yes, there are times to fake it and let your abilities catch up, because people do judge you by how you present yourself.

But God doesn't.

God knows you inside and out. He knows every secret, every hidden thought and desire. When you come before him, you don't need to fake righteousness, you don't need to pretend. You can be who you are, mistakes and all, laying it out with complete transparency. He knows. He knew the instant it happened. Don't try to impress God, just be who you are.

Confess everything and don't hold back. He forgives, and only asks that you are truly sorry and will change.

What if you're not completely sorry? What if you were mean to someone and still feel like they deserved it?

God knows. He *knows*! So be honest with him - confess that you don't feel remorse, even though you were in the wrong. Ask him to work in your heart so you'll let go of the resentment that's making you act mean or hateful. Ask him to change your feelings. Then let him. Stop resisting forgiveness. Quit hoarding your anger, stoking it with resentful thoughts, collecting situations that fortify your wall of resentment.

I promise you, as long as you look for things to "justify"

your bad feelings, you will find them. So stop looking! Let the hurtful things that happen pass you by. Don't grab them, saying "See? I told you so!" to anyone who listens.

Be honest with God. Identify the problem areas. Give them to him and live in faith and trust.

He knows everything about you and loves you regardless! He sees the person you are now and the person you can become and he loves you.

Today, when you come before God, tell him how you really feel. Don't hold back. Then ask for His help and surrender. Write those things down you are giving to him, then burn, shred or otherwise destroy them. It's between you and God.

62 - Comfort Verses

CHAPTER TWENTY-SIX
HOPE AND A FUTURE

For I know the plans I have for you," says the Lord.
"They are plans for good and not for disaster,
to give you a future and a hope."
Jeremiah 29:11 (NLT)

After my divorce I felt hopeless. I'd always been a planner, a goal-setter, an achiever. It had defined me. Divorce happened and I found I had no vision and couldn't form a plan. I felt like I'd lost a significant part of my identity at a time when I'd already taken a body blow in that department.

Being unable to picture a future left me scared and uncertain, hopeless and depressed. When I read this verse it gave me such comfort. Even though *I* couldn't see a future, God could. He had a plan for me, one designed to help me thrive and prosper. He has a plan for you, too.

God's intention is for us to be the best we can be, serving him, trusting him and moving forward. He is our hope and he guides us through the times when we can't see the path.

"But I'll take the hand of those who don't know
the way, who can't see where they're going.
I'll be a personal guide to them, directing
them through unknown country.
I'll be right there to show them what roads to take,
make sure they don't fall into the ditch.
These are the things I'll be doing for them— sticking

with them, not leaving them for a minute."
Isaiah 42:16 (TMB)

When you talk to God today, ask him about the plans he has for you. Write down some of the things that come into your mind.

CHAPTER TWENTY-SEVEN
GOD'S GRACE IS OUR FREEDOM

*For the grace of God has been revealed,
bringing salvation to all people.
And we are instructed to turn from godless
living and sinful pleasures.
We should live in this evil world with
wisdom, righteousness, and
devotion to God, while we look forward with hope to
that wonderful day when the glory of our great
God and Savior, Jesus Christ, will be revealed.
He gave his life to free us from every kind of sin, to cleanse us,
and to make us his very own people,
totally committed to doing good deeds.
Titus 2:11-13 (NLT)*

Why aren't we in charge of our own salvation?

Some people think we should get to heaven by being a good person. How good would you have to be to earn heaven? Who would set the standard?

What about a person who gives money to feed the hungry and shelter the poor but abuses his child? Is that a good person? How about someone who is fun to be with and nice to everyone, but submits a false insurance claim?

Okay, false insurance claim, you say you might be able to excuse that... What about the Bernie Madoffs? What if Bernie had given 90% of his stolen loot to charity? Would that make him good? Good enough to get to heaven?

The problem is there are too many variables in human calculations. And things change. If people were in charge, would it be like taxes? Looking for loopholes? Unsure of the requirements?

What if you were given the keys to heaven but you had to give away all your money? Or sacrifice your livelihood? Or your children?

What is the cost of eternal life in the hereafter?

Priceless.

You could never pay enough. You don't have enough resources, enough valuable things. It's out of your reach.

But what if it was a gift?

There it is, sitting on the table. It's got your name on it. If you claim it, it's yours. If you don't, you'll never know.

If you have claimed God's gift of eternal life you already know that although it's based on grace, it changes you. You can't accept Jesus into your heart without a transformation in your behavior and your attitude. God wants you to live with wisdom, righteousness and devotion. Not as the world does, with greed and self-interest, but with love and compassion toward others.

You can do this because, as a child of God, you are clean. Past sins, no matter how bad, are gone.

You are not your sins, *you are not divorce,* you are not your mistakes.

You are one of God's people, committed to him and doing good deeds because it's who you are.

You are an important part of his Kingdom, no matter what has happened in your life.

It's quite a gift.

Make sure you don't leave it on the table.

68 - Comfort Verses

CHAPTER TWENTY-EIGHT
COMFORT ENOUGH TO SHARE

*All praise to God, the Father of our Lord Jesus Christ.
God is our merciful Father and the source of all comfort.
He comforts us in all our troubles so
that we can comfort others.
When they are troubled, we will be able to give them
the same comfort God has given us
2 Corinthians 1:3-4 (NLT)*

We're at the end of the four-week series of comfort verses. I hope you've found comfort, peace and even some challenges along the way. I chose to end with this verse because it reminds me how God is our Father and the source of all our comfort.

I also like the idea of God comforting us so we can turn around and extend that same comfort to others. It's what inspired me to tell my story and coach others who face loss, life-crisis and major changes. And it falls right in line with God's commandment to love and care for each other.

*"I have loved you even as the Father has loved me.
Remain in my love. When you obey my commandments,
you remain in my love, just as I obey my Father's
commandments and remain in his love. I have told
you these things so that you will be filled with my joy.
Yes, your joy will overflow! This is my commandment:
Love each other in the same way I have loved you."
John 15:9-12 (NLT)*

Even though I may not know you, I picture you in my mind as I write. Even though our circumstances may be different, I have compassion for your pain. I've known pain, and I understand.

As I mentioned earlier, I lost all hope for a while and with God's help I've come back to a place that is better than anywhere else I've been. My life today is not perfect, not without troubles, but I've learned to be joyful and give thanks, trust God and live fully.

Obeying His commandments is not easy, and I'm not perfect. However I've seen the effects of committing to His word in my life and the lives of those around me, and I know it's not a casual request from God. It's important and our obedience allows him to accomplish things that are magnificent.

I hope these 28 days have given you assurance that you are not alone, you are loved and God has a plan to bless you no matter how old you are or in what circumstances you find yourself.

You can rebuild a life that's the best you've ever had. His Word gives you the tools you need to do that.

Now it's up to you.

AFTERWORD

Perhaps you've been reading this, not sure if you have accepted Jesus as your personal Savior. If you want the life discussed in these verses, you only need to do three things:

ADMIT that you need God, you've made mistakes (or sinned) and ask him to forgive your sins.

> *If we confess our sins to him, he is faithful and just to forgive us and to cleanse us from every wrong.*
> 1 John 1:9 (NLT)

BELIEVE Jesus died to pay the price for your sins and that he rose from the dead and is alive today. He is the only way to salvation.

> *If you confess with your mouth, 'Jesus is Lord,' and believe in your heart that God raised him from the dead, you will be saved.*
> Romans 10:9 (NIV)

> *Salvation is found in no one else [Jesus], for there is no other name by which we must be saved.*
> Acts 4:12, (NIV)

> *Jesus is the only One who can save people. His name is the only power in the world that has been given to save people. We must be saved through him.*

Acts 4:12 (New Century Version)

ACCEPT God's gift to you and start your new life fresh, clean and renewed. Let him transform you.

> *For it is by grace you have been saved, through faith—*
> *and this is not from yourselves, it is the gift of God—*
> *not by works, so that no one can boast.*
> Ephesians 2:8, 9 (NIV)

> *To all who received him, he gave the right to*
> *become children of God.*
> *All they needed to do was to*
> *trust him to save them.*
> *All those who believe this are reborn!—*
> *not a physical rebirth...*
> *but from the will of God.*
> John 1:12,13 (The Living Bible)

You can pray a simple prayer, such as:

I know I'm a sinner. I believe Jesus, Son of the living God, died for my sins when he died on the cross. I accept God's gift of salvation. I want him to be the Lord of my life.

Amen.

If you do this and want to tell me about it, I'd love to hear. If my book of Comfort Verses helped or comforted you, please consider telling a few friends about it.

Please visit my website: DivorceisnotDestiny.com to contact me (Lynn@DivorceisnotDestiny.com)

My book, *Divorce is not Destiny,* is also available, with more details on the website.

Blessings and joy to you.

Lynn